LOOK AT ME A LIVING TESTIMONY

ONE MAN'S JOURNEY FROM DARKNESS TO LIGHT
(A collection of spiritual poems for all occassions)

Printed and Bound in the United States of America
Published and Distributed by:
Professional Publishing House

Cover Design: Kevin Allen
Formatting: Professional Publishing House

First Printing, December 2009
10 9 8 7 6 5 4 3 2 1

ISBN# 978-0-9824292-5-9

Library of Congress Cataloging-in-Publication Data

Professional Publishing House
1425 W. Manchester Blvd., Suite B
Los Angeles, CA 90047
www.milliganbooks.com
drrosie@aol.com
(323) 750-3592

LOOK AT ME A LIVING TESTIMONY

ONE MAN'S JOURNEY FROM DARKNESS TO LIGHT
(A collection of spiritual poems for all occassions)

CLAYBORNE BROWN, JR. AKA "MR. CLAY"

This book is dedicated to anyone who may be doing drugs, whatever their drug of choice may be, and my deepest prayer is that this book might be an inspiration for them to get some help before it is too late. This book is also dedicated to anyone that has been chosen to do something and you know you have been chosen … by all means, do it, because, "Today well lived makes yesterday a dream of happiness and tomorrow a vision of hope."

Acknowledgements

To God I Give All the praise, honor, and glory, because when I needed Him, He was there:

- 1970—head injury, brain damage
- 1975 & 1976—right knee surgery, could have lost leg
- 1995—open heart surgery … He is still with me today.
- A special family that is very close to my heart—Debra Ecung and her husband, Ernest Ecung, Sr.—helped me get into the Open Door Mission Drug Program.
- Ernest Ecung, II, and Eric Ecung—were there when I needed moral support, and they are still in my corner today.
- Annie B. Davis—my big sister in Christ.

About The Author

Clayborne Brown, Jr. aka "Mr. Clay"

Born on September 1, 1952, in Houston, Texas, with a natural gift from God to write poetry and cook (he excels in both).

The author moved to Los Angeles, California, in September of 2000. He attends Calvary Baptist Church, L.A., under the leadership of Rev. Virgil V. Jones. For the past seven years he has been a faithful member of Calvary and was the sound technician for a few years. Mr. Clay has a God-given gift for helping people, which has made him an excellent caregiver. His cooking, caregiving, and writing poetry comes from the heart with great care.

Without going to deep into my past life, I used drugs—crack cocaine was my drug of choice. I thank God that I have been clean and sober eleven-plus years. October 26, 2008, will be twelve years. One day when I was at work, my employer told me she knew I was doing drugs and wanted to assist me in getting some help. Even though I told her I was not using or doing drugs, I asked her if I could take a rain check on her offer on one condition. She said, "Yes, and what is the condition?" My response was, "Should I come to realize that I do have a problem with, drugs, can I come back and accept your offer?" and she said yes. I completed my work, fixed a lunch to take with me, got paid, and left.

Three days later, I called her and asked if her offer was still on the table. She said it was and told me to come over to the house and she would find a place for me to go to get help.

When I left her house and before I went to work at my regular job, I got high. (I was working for a dry cleaner on a shirt press.) I got hungry and tried to eat some chicken and rice, but could not, because it tasted like crack cocaine. I took a bite out of an oatmeal cookie, but could not eat it, because it tasted like crack cocaine. I got a peppermint candy, tasted it, and it tasted like crack cocaine. I even tried to drink some water, but could not, because it tasted like crack cocaine. I knew then that was God at work, because four different things all tasted like one (crack cocaine). God allowed me to see my reflection on a grey brick wall as if I were looking in a mirror. When I spoke my upper lip went one way and my bottom lip went the opposite.

My equilibrium was off balance. When I took one step forward and my foot came down, it was three steps to the right or left of me. Somehow I ended up at the Open Door Mission. I graduated October 26, 1996, and the rest is history.

Look at me … a living testimony.

Foreword

Re: Clayborne Brown, Jr.

A poet by any other name is still...

I am honored to have been asked to write something about the author. I have known Clayborne for just under ten years. In that span, went from obscurity to visibility showcasing his talents. He has wonderful culinary skills preparing edibles to meet the approval of the most scrutinizing of qualified masticators. He has exceptional creative writing skills preparing sonnets and limericks that compare to the likes of Langston Hughes, Maya Angelou and Paul Lawrence Dunbar. He has a pure and righteous heart allowing him not only the pleasure of having his gift but also the capacity to share his gift. I have witnessed him giving his previous work *"How You Like Me Now?"* to countless individuals free of charge. His reason, "God told me to." I believe that is why his first writing has met renowned status and this next one promises to achieve the same acclaim.

As I look to finalize my thoughts, I refer to his name. Clay is appropriate for his lips of clay have been anointed to share his story (his own) and His Story (God's). Born is appropriate for he was born for this purpose and born again for His (God's) purpose. The "E" that tags along at the end of his first name suggests the excitement one feels whenever in his presence. Brown, a surname to be sure, fits so well as he in one whose skin has been kissed by the Father's sun (and Son). It is a pleasure to serve as his pastor and recommend this reading for your enjoyment. Praise God!

Pastor Virgil Jones

Foreword

Writers have been inspired by the words spoken by Jesus, "But I, when I am lifted up from the earth, will draw all men unto myself" (John 12:32). And, "With God all things are possible" was one of the passages from scripture that Mr. Brown spoke to my spirit for encouragement. I have treasured the penned words of this great spiritual vessel. God's spirit flows sweet melodies of comfort through the inspired words written by Mr. Clayborne Brown, Jr. This spirit filled author has filters' the stories of hope, sweet dishes, (A true chief he is) caring, love, mercy and grace in the Lord. God's Grace is sufficient. I am encouraged and sure of one thing that God has smiled on him and Mr. Brown, Jr., is loved by many readers in God's great vineyard of enlarging ones territory. "How You Like Me Now," has now soared into the minds and hearts of those God chose to reap the benefits of treasures there hidden for the masses. I take great honor in sharing my thoughts of this true lover of God. A man of God that has shared by tears and help to wipe away my sorrows and for that I say Thanks be to God for such a motivator as Mr. Clayborne Brown, Jr.

Evangelist, Beverly Woodard

From The Author

I said a prayer for you today and I know God must have heard,

I felt the answer in my heart … Although He never spoke a word.

I did not ask for wealth of fame, I knew you would not mind,

I asked Him to send you treasures from afar … The more lasting kind.

I asked that He would be near you at the start of every day, to grant you health and blessings as you go on your way.

I asked Him to give you joy and peace in all things great and small, but it was His Grace that I prayed for most al all.

… Yes, God has blessed me to share these poems with you, some may be long and some may be short,

Read them closely, take them dearly and take them to heart.

I knew God gives life and he blesses you and me,

Each and every time he wakes us on a new day to see.

Today is special and you have a blessing coming your way, so give God thanks for blessing you to see this day.

Be happy not sad and may there be no inner strife, as you accept God's will, while you travel this road in life.

Because God has been good to you and me, and His blessings we can truly see.

TABLE OF CONTENTS

Just For You

"God in His love does some of His greatest work and sends some of His greatest blessing through Mothers."

Even though it cannot be said in a line or two,
God has blessed me to write this poem for you.

Life is like a Garden and friendship is like a flower,
that blooms and grows to beauty with the sunshine and a shower.

Lovely are the blossoms that are tended to with care,
by a mother who work to make this place more fair.

There is no one who is thoughtful and oh so dear,
for making life more brighter with love throughout the year.

God had blessed you with a heart that knows his word,
Yet … when you speak of life experiences, you are heard.

That is why God gives you a smile even when things are not going right,
And a special spirit that dwells within you is a heavenly delight.

For these qualities you are thought about with love on this day of all days.

… Here's to you with my greatest wish today, tomorrow and always, may
God's love and peace surround you today and throughout the year.

And may God bless you with peace and comfort when no one is near,
… Yes, my heart and love goes out to you in a Godly way

From Clayborne Brown, Jr., … Happy Mother's Day.

For Goodness and Mercy

The Bible to me is a treasure house where I can always find,
whatever I need from day to day, heart, soul and mind.
God's word if understood can keep us free from strife,
when it is obeyed, it brings us joy and nourishes our life.
Consider what the Lord has done through those who have shown you love,
then thank them for their faithful deeds and blessings from above.

Now, when my thoughts and the words are on one accord,
then the words of my mouth honor Christ my Lord.
... The child of God who reads the word,
heeds to the message he has heard.
Will grow in grace from day to day,
and share with others on life's way.

I know God lived as a man, and he understands our need for grace,
yet, He is never far from whatever trails we face.
... There is a treasure you can own,
that is greater than a crown or throne.
A conscience good with to live,
that only God himself can give.
... Lord, whenever we are afraid we will put our trust in you,
to lead, protect, and guide our way and help us make it through.

Trust Him

If you are discouraged and you think you are lost,
and upon life's billow you are tossed.

Count your many blessings … Name them one-by-one,
and you will be surprised to what God has done.

… If God is prompting you today to help someone in need,
do not hesitate, the time is short, tomorrow is not guaranteed.

We as Christians have been gifted by grace from God above,
and we are equipped to build and strengthen the church in faith and in love.

If we read the Bible and obey God's principles within,
it will transform our lives and turn us from sin.

More precious than gold is God's word to me,
and much better than pearls from the deep blue sea.

Because in God's word, I take great delight,
and it is my joy every day and every night.

… If we spend time in secret with Jesus alone,
we will have time to be holy, because the world rushes on.

So start early today to run in the race that Christians are told that they can win, then wait on God for the strength He will give, then lay aside every known sin.

No Greater Love

© Clayborne Brown, Jr. 2009

When reading God's word take special care,
to find the rich treasures that are hidden there.

Because the Bible gives us all we need to live our lives for God each
day, but it will not work if we do not do what the pages say.

To serve God with a heart of love is all He ask of you,
and He will give you help when doing the work He has for you to do.

When faced with trials from without and tempted from within,
count upon God for strength to turn away from sin.

Cause the Christian life is more than
just a prayer of faith from the past,
it is dedicating everyday to live for Christ and what will last.

We should not presume to know what is best when we pray,
but, we should think about what honors
God then seek His will and way.

As an example of good to all mankind,
ask God to show you how to let your light shine.

Because when you put all your trust in the Savior of Light,
He can and will bring hope in the darkest of night.

... If you are tempted to deny God's goodness, love and grace,
look to the cross of Calvary where Christ took your place.

Know that God's word is like refreshing rain
that waters crops and seed,
and it brings new life to open hearts and meets us in our need.

... That is why God's answer was not detected
when Jesus came to earth,
... No one expected greatness from a child of a lowly birth.

I Will

Be still my child and know that I am God,
wait thou patiently … I know the path you till trod.

Fear not, Father not, do not think to run and hide,
for I thy hope and strength am waiting by thy side.

… Fellowship with other Christians,
strengthen us when we are weak,
reprimands when we are sinning helps when God's will we seek.

Start early to run in the race that
Christians are told they can win,
but wait on the Lord for the strength
He will give, then lay aside every sin.

We as Christians have been gifted by God above,
equipped to build and strengthen the church in faith and love.

When Jesus took a servant's towel, his honor … He set aside,
because he was showing us how to serve
and how to conquer pride.

… Always give your best to the Master,
yes give Him first place in your heart,
give Him first place in your service,
so he can consecrate every part.

With gladness go forth each day expecting
to serve and claim,
the happiness that service gives when it is
rendered in God's name.

Yes, we were once held by Satan's chains,
imprisoned by our own sins,
then Jesus Christ delivered us and made us new within.

Now if we keep doing what is right
and serve God everyday,
we will not fear what other people think, do or say.

... True greatness does not lie with those
who strive for worldly fame,
instead, it lies with those who choose to serve in Jesus name.

If we trust in Christ to save us, then we will enjoy the new birth,
because we cannot earn our way to heaven,
by word, work or worth.

How Excellent

At the name of Jesus falling prostrate at his feet,
King of Kings in heaven we will crown Him when our journey is complete.

The wonder of creation speaks to everyone in different ways,
because of his handiwork ... Those who love and know Him give praise.

Help me sing a joyful song for those bowed down with care,
a song of hope and freedom for those in dark despair.

Everything false will disappear when wave-notes fill my ear,
open my ears so I may hear voices of truth that thou sendest clear.

Take control of my words today, may they speak of your great love,
may the story of your grace turn some heart to you above.

When our lives are heaven laden cold and bleak as winter is long,
stir the embers in our heart Lord, make your flame burn bright and strong.

So if I meet someone with a Christ like touch,
I can bless so many and help so much.

Think About It

As we strive to do the will of God and struggle to succeed,
we must not fail to recognize that God's strength is all we need.
If we meet the Savior each day in a quiet secret place,
we might grow a little stronger with a fresh supply of grace.
I do not know what method the Lord provides for me,
but I do know, all my needs are met so graciously.
Even though God wipe the tears from weeping eyes,
He still cares for every soul that cries.

Because he knows our burdens, our pain, and our crosses,
the things that hurt … Our trials and our losses.
Now … If you do a deed of kindness though the end you may not
see, it may reach, like widening ripples down a long eternity.
To love your neighbor as yourself is not an easy task,
God will still show his love through you, if you only ask.
Because he promised in His holy word,
our faintest heart felt cry will always be heard.

… Ask God to give you a loving heart, a will to give and share,
a soft prayer to show how much you really care.
Because a careless word may kindle strife,
a cruel word may wreck a life.
A timely word may lessen stress,
and a loving word may heal and even bless.
So when you see someone in need,

know that love demands a loving deed.
Don't just you love him true,
prove it by the deeds you do.

Praise Him

As I give thanks and my heart kneels to pray,
I ask God to keep me, guide me, and go with me today.
Because into our lives come things that break the routine,
things we had not planned on and the unforeseen.
The unexpected little joys that are scattered along the way,
even success we did not count on … Or a successful day.

… The earth is the Lord's and the fullness thereof,
it speaks of His goodness and sings about His love.
Each day at dawn, I lift my heart up high,
and raise my eyes to the infinite sky.
To see the night vanish and a new day is born,

… I see the birds and I hear them sing on the wings of the morn.
I see the dew glisten in it's crystal like splendor,
with the touch of God that is gentle and tender.
Because God has wrapped up the night and softly put it away,
and he has hung out the sun to herald a brand new day.

Easter Morning

Dear Lord, please be merciful to me
... My sin has grieved your heart,
grant me your strength a new so I can make a fresh start.
Speak to my heart and give me compassion,
let your love flow through me today,
So if I see someone hurting, I will know what to do and say.
I pray that nothing will take the
strength of Christ that is in me,
because the joy of His presence will always be.
Even though I am not worthy of such a divine guest,
I pray daily that my spirit longs for you to it's best.

... Christ did not come to shield us from the grief and pain of life,
but those who have peace inside can thrive within the strife.
We are to honor our Savior by helping
when and wherever we can,
because we have Jesus who always went
about doing good as a man.
... Help us Lord, to be a lifeline to a dying world today,
as we bring hope to hopeless people when we tell them that Christ is the way.
No one knew that a child born of such a lowly birth,
was God's answer for all mankind,
made flesh when he came to earth.

On Easter Morning, I hear voices singing,
"Lord you have risen today,
you are not in the tomb," the stone has been rolled away.
Through you my life has been made new,
because you rose Easter Morning to show us, we can rise too.
Now there is no stone and we must be reborn,
just like you rose that Easter morn.

Just Because

You cannot hide your sins from God because he knows what is in your heart,
yet, confession is the quickest way to make a brand new start.

So hold fast to Christ, because he has the will to see you through,
and if you keep on keeping on, your strength He will renew.

God sees our ways and knows our hearts ... From Him we cannot hide,
because external righteousness cannot save us, for He knows what is inside.

Even though you cannot earn your way into heaven ... The wages for sinning is death,
Jesus is still longing to save you from sin ... So don't wait until you draw your last breath.

◆ ◆ ◆

True wisdom is in living near Jesus everyday,
and true wisdom is walking where He shall lead the way.

So when fear and worry test your faith and anxious thoughts assail,
remember that God is in control and He will not fail.

That is why I would walk in the dark with God than go alone in the light,
and I would walk by faith with Him than go along by sight.

Yes, the Lord wants more than platitudes from those for whom He died,
because He longs for us to know His love, and in that love abide.

What Would Virgil Say?

You are called with a holy calling … The light of the world to be,
to life the lamp of the Savior, that others His light may see.

Lord, grant me grace throughout this day,
to walk the straight and narrow way.

To do whatever in thy sight, is good and perfect, just and right.
Father give me sensitivity to people in their grief and pain,
to weep with them and show your love in ways that words cannot attain."

"Open my eyes Lord, to people around me, help me to see them as you do above,
give me the wisdom and strength to take action so others may see the depth of your love.

Oh, how great is the gift that Jesus gave to me!
He lived a perfect life, and he died upon a tree.

Not for me alone has he paid the price,
But for all the world … For his sacrifice."

"No one could enter heaven, our many sins stood in the way,
So God in his love sent Jesus … For He alone sins depth could pay.

Turn your eyes upon Jesus, look full in His wonderful face, and the things of earth will grow dim in the light of His glory and grace.

Remember, it is not what I achieve nor if I gain wealth of fame, the only thing I must be certain of is … Have I put my trust in Jesus name."

"Trails makes us think … Thinking makes us wise and wisdom makes life profitable."

THE ONE

Lord, teach us from your holy word all error to discern,
and by your spirits light help us from Satan's snares to turn.

Give us grace to trust you when life's burdens seem too much to bear,
dispel the darkness with new hope and help us rise above despair.

I know we are called with a holy calling, the light of the world to be,
to lift up the lamp of the gospel that others the light may see.

There may be times when our minds are in doubt,
and we ask ourselves, what is this faith all about?

It is then when we should remember that God is real like the Bible declares,
... Yet, we can trust and believe Him cause we know He cares.

Now ... The longer we live, the more that we know,
because as we age and through time wisdom will show.

... Who knows what good some word we might say,
could do for someone who has wandered away.

I know that my life is a painting created by God ... I have nothing to boast,
but to reflect the image of Christ to the world is what I desire the most.

... Whatever task you find to do, regardless if it is big or small,
perform it well with all your might, because there is one who sees it all.

Bless Me

Almighty, matchless, glorious God, inhabiting eternity,
I bow to you and give you praise, in awe that you can live in me.

There is so much I cannot see, my eye sight is far to dim,
but come what may … I will trust and leave it all to Him.

Those who draw upon God's love show love in all they do,
because unfailing is God's matchless love
… So kind, so pure and so true.

To fear the Lord means giving Him reverence, trust and awe,
as we acknowledge His sovereignty and submit to His law.

To follow Christ we must let go of all that we hold dear,
and once we have denied ourselves, or gains become more clear.

So, reach out in Jesus name with helping hands of care,
to those who are in need and caught in life's despair.

Remember, if we sing songs of praise to God through tears,
we will grow in grace through all our years.

Because the gifts that we may give and deeds that we do,
will honor Christ when self if given too.

He's Not Dead

Today Christ says "*Come follow me! … Look not to yesterday, fresh grace you will need to do my will, trust me and obey.*"

… Oh how wonderful it is to know he who watches from above,
will always keep us sheltered in His ever present love.

When a crisis looms before you, do not face it on your own,
seek advice from godly counsel, and take it to Gods throne.

The choice we make determines our eternal destination,
one leads to everlasting life, the other condemnation.

My life … Today I yield O Lord to thee,
a channel for your love and grace to be.

Use me just as you will I humbly pray,
to point some soul unto the living way.

Help me remember what you did to set me free,
and thank you for dying for me on the cross of Calvary.

You got up on the third day with all power in your hand,
to share new life and salvation was bright to every woman, child
and man.

We want to do great things to glorify your name,
because you transformed us by your power and we will never be the same.

Give us wisdom Lord to provide the proper atmosphere,
to lead our children in your ways by what they see and hear.

Because there is never a night or day,
when God does not hear us when we pray.

… There is no time and there is no place,
when we are beyond God's love and his grace.

Love and Happiness

Your love, oh God would spare no pain to conquer death and win,
because you sent your only son to die, and to rescue us from sin.

Now we have hope cause Christ has risen
... Death was conquered by your son,
bless us now to share that message with
someone hurting or a grieving one.

To observe God's love from afar is only a passing delight,
but when we experience Christ presence,
our darkness is turned into light.

What we possess is not our own it all comes from God,
because He sustains the gift of life,
its labor and the reward.

... When you are walking with the Lord,
the future is always bright,
and it matters not what comes our way when faith replaces sight.

Because the spirit gives us unity and love for everyone,
for we are members of God's family when we accept His son.

... The stories in the word of God are there for us to see,
... How God has worked in people's lives throughout all history.

Just For You

What is Mother's Day?

Mother's Day is celebrating motherhood and what it means to be the one who is the very heart of the home and the family.

Mother's Day is celebrating all the love that is so often unexpressed and finding the special words and ways that will help say it best …

… Mother's Day is celebrating everything that loving mother's do
… Yes, the cherished and remembered things that will last a lifetime through.

… Most of all, this day was meant for women just like you.

Happy Mother's Day

A Mother's Comfort

You have a heart that hears every spoken and unspoken need,
and the godly wisdom to know when to lead.

You have eyes that reflect more joy you could ever find,
and arms to hold love ones ... but never to bind.

Even though you have a smile to share when thing are not just right,
God has blessed you with a spirit that can soothe, inspire and even be a delight.

... My dear lady, you are such a blessing to everyone around you,
it is always a comfort when you are near.

Here's wishing that the blessings of God's love and peace,
always surround you on Mother's day and throughout the year.

Happy Mother's Day

On Your Birthday

"Here's thinking of you and thanking God for making you a beautiful part of His world."

Roses may be red and violets may be blue,
there is something I must tell you.

"You are thought about with a warm and tender love,
yes baby, the kind that comes from God above.

... I know that there is a living and loving God,
He rules the universe, the sea and the sky, for Him nothing is hard.

He holds all creatures in the palm of His hand,
And He can put infinity in one tiny grain of sand.

He made the seasons winter, summer, fall and spring,
and He put rhythm into every created thing.

When He take the stars in as He put the night away,
He hangs the sun out slowly with the break of day.

No artist can alter His perfect master plan,
because His mighty handiwork defies even the skill of man.

What better things are there to prove his holy bring,
than the wonders all around us, that are ours for the seeing.

Happy Birthday My Love

Only You

My dear lady, if there was one face I wanted to see each day my whole life through,
My search would be over, because your smile makes a difference in everything that I do.

... When I search for companionship, honesty and a place to be myself, I met you.

Baby, if there was one touch I longed to feel and one voice I longed to hear,
it would be you, because you are so sweet and so dear.

... When I searched for goodness and the challenge to expand myself, I met you.

If there was one joy and one love from which I never wanted to part.
You are that someone special in my world, my life and most of all my heart,

... When I search for satisfaction and someone to bring balance to my life, I met you.

... Here's to you baby and I truly thank God for making you a beautiful part of this world and my life.

Happy Birthday

In His Presence

If we hide our shining light and not reflect God's son,
then how will people in sin's night be guided, helped and won?

If you are feeling alone, unworthy
and wish for a kind loving friend,
remember that God longs to show you a love that will never end.

At times our path may be rough or steep
and the way is hard to see,
we ask God why is life unfair? He answers … "Follow Me."

Living for the Lord and to fear Him each day,
best prepares the soul for the stormy way.

Because the sea of life around you may even roar,
but when you look to Jesus, you hear it no more.

Now if the world is in turmoil, in Him I find rest,
because when I'm with Jesus my spirit is blessed.

Yes, Christ builds the church and makes it strong by using you and me.
… If we do our part, the world … His love will truly see.

For Goodness and Mercy

Gods words if understood can keep us free from strife,
when it is obeyed it will bring us joy and nourish our life.

If we consider what the Lord has done t
hrough those who have shown us love,
we should thank them for their faithful deeds and blessings from above.

Now ... when my thoughts and the word are on one accord,
then the words of my mouth honor Christ my Lord.

The bible to me is a treasure house where I can always find,
whatever I need from day to day for heart, soul and mind.

Because He walked earth as a man, and
He understands our need for grace,

so believe you me, there is a treasure you can own,
that is greater than a crown or throne ...

... A conscience so good with which one can live.
That only God himself can give.

Yes, Christ builds the church and makes it strong by using you and me.
... If we do our part, the world ... His love will truly see.

Are You Listening?

© Clayborne Brown, Jr. 2009

As we join our heart and hands together, faithful to the Lord command,
we hold each other to God's standard and all that the truth demand.

By God's design there lies in wait for you,
important work that no one else can do.

Just like the planets find their paths through space,
we must grown to fill our proper place.

My hands perform His bidding, my feet run in His ways,
my eyes see Jesus only, my lips speak forth his praise.

I know that God is watching, always present everywhere,
with joy and patience, He is waiting for our prayer.

... Controlling other people lives is not a Godly trait,
but serving other people needs is what the Lord consider great.

He Lives

© Clayborne Brown, Jr. 2009

When our problems overwhelm us, God wants us to look to Him,
because He will provide the right solutions,
and light our path that was dim.

He sent the Holy Spirit after Christ ascended from this earth,
this we know cause we are here to share the
good news about the second birth.

... God often meets our deepest need with the help we gain from others,
like the caring members of His church, our sisters and our brothers.

Afflictions may test us yet, they will not destroy,
because just a glimpse of God's love turns them all to joy.

The more about Jesus, that I know,
the more of His grace to others I will show.

... Christ took each sin, each pain and each loss,
to save us by the power of the Cross.

... When you are reborn ... Made new in Christ
it should be plain for all of see,
That God has changed us from within and placed us in his family.

Did You Know?

It is one thing to read the Bible through and through,
Another to read, to learn, and to do.

Some read it as their duty once a week,
But no instructions from the Bible do they seek.

Some read to bring themselves into repute,
By showing others how they can dispute.

There are those who read it because their neighbors do,
To see how long it will take them to read it through.

Some read it for the wonders that are there,
How David killed a lion and a bear.

One may read with daddy glasses on his head,
And see things just like his daddy said.

Others read it with uncommon care,
Hoping to find some contradictions there.

DID YOU KNOW? …

Some people read the Bible to prove a pre-adopted creed,
Yet they understand very little of what they read.

Even though there are many people who read the Bible right,
There are still some who read it out of spite.

So read the Bible prayerfully and you will see,
Whatever is right God's word will agree.

... Because of what the early Bible prophets wrote,
We find that Christ and His apostles quote.

So trust no creed that troubles you to recall,
What has been penned by one, and verified by all.

God Is

As we travel up and down life's road,
It may seem to be very hard,
It really isn't if you believe and trust in God.
Even though there may be things we may not understand,
Fear not, fret not, because God has the master plan,
God is the only one who blesses us from day to day,
And I have learned to abide by and do as He says.
God is the one who really cares for you,
Because He is always there to see you through.
Yes ... He knows our hearts, our minds, and our every step,
And He is always there when we need His help.

Please Tell Someone

My friend, I stand in judgment now,
And I feel that you are the blame somehow.
We walked together on earth day by day,
... Never did you point or show me the way.
You knew the Lord in truth and in glory,
But you never told me the story.

Even though my knowledge was very dim,
You could have led me safe to Him.
Yes, we lived together down on earth,
And you never told me about the second birth.
You taught me many things, this is true,
Yet, I called you friend, and I even trusted you.

We walked by day and talked by night,
And you never took the time to lead me to the light.
You let me live to love and to die,
... Thinking I would never live on high.

I have learned now, though it may be too late,
You could have kept me from this fate.
... As I now come up to the end,
I know I cannot call you my friend.

I will not depend upon you, another person, but I will tell someone else,
Because I have learned to know and love the Lord for myself,

4/16/94

Today

On this day, I will try to live through this day only.
Not tackling my whole life's problems at once.
On this day, I will try to be happy, realize my happiness.
Does not depend on what others do or say, or what happens.
Around me. Happiness is a result of being at peace with myself.
On this day, I will try to adjust myself to what is, and,
Not force everything to adjust to my own desires, I will accept.
My family, my friends, my business, my circumstances, as
they come.
On this day, I will do at least one thing I do not want to do.
And I will perform a small act of love for my neighbor.
On this day, I will not be afraid to be happy; I will enjoy what
is good, what is beautiful, and what is lovely in life.
On this day, I will have a quiet time of meditation, wherein I
shall think of God, myself, and my neighbor; I shall relax
and seek truth.
On this day, I will accept myself and live to the best of my
ability.
On this day, I choose to believe that I can live this one day.

9/1/96

Obedience

If I gained the world, would I lose my Savior, or would
my life be worth living for today?
Would my yearning heart find rest, peace, and comfort
in the things that would soon pass away?
When I read by Bible and meditate on what God's
Word said,
I would learn how to fight temptation from the world
and live a life that is spirit-led.

There is wisdom to be learned, and there is only one
true way to grow.
So I humble myself, listen like a child, as I learn what
God would have me know.
If my path for any reason should be dark on any given
day.
My faith is in God and by all means I let God have his
way.

I have enough faith to know the sun will surely shine.
And because of His love, He has planned your way and,
of course, mine.
Yes, God really does have a plan for you and me.
When we listen and we are obedient, it will be so easy
to see.

God is there to help us, guide us, and He is with us
each and every step of the way.
Keeping His promise … reminding us daily that His
grace is sufficient for any day.
Daily He is working to instill.
In our heart and mind His perfect and eternal will.
It is said, He will return to judge the world someday.
Are you prepared for Him to come, or … are you hoping for a
delay?

11/15/97

Here and Now

I have had headaches, and I have shed tears,
I have had gloomy days and fruitless years.

To thee, or Lord, I give thanks, because I now know,
Those were some of the things that helped me grow.

You always let me know that You were there,
Because of answered prayers, You showed how much you care.

... Jesus is all the world to me ... my life, my joy, my all in all,
He is my strength from day to day ... without Him I would fall.

Father, open our eyes so we may see,
The love, the mercy, and grace that comes from Thee.

In faith I pray that You will fill our soul with a love that is divine,
So our heart will be more like Thine.

No matter what I do, where I go, I cannot hide,
When I need strength, I come to you, my spiritual guide.

Even though I know Jesus is coming back to claim the church
as His wife,
I know goodness and mercy follow me each day of my life.

3/28/97

God's Love

Even though it cannot be said in a line or two,
God has bless me to share these words with you,
I have come to the life of Jesus, He is my Lord and,
My friend, His power flows though me,
this message I now extend.

When you are bold in your witness,
by sharing with the lost God's Word,
Jesus will honor your service and the lost will be stirred,
Because He whose right was heaven's glory,
chose to serve here on earth below,

Leaving us a clear example of the love He would have us show,
God sent His son to die for us, no other life would do,
Trust in Christ daily, accept and use the gift He has given you,
When your fears seem so large and,
you look for proffer that God is near.
It is then He says: have faith, my child, and do not fear,
His love is freely given, yet He supplies our every need.
So let's share that love as the spirit leads.
... It is a love of caring when the world cries.

Because that love is having compassion with Christ-like eyes.
There may come a time when things are difficult and you do
not try or show that you care.
That is when you should remember that God said,
Love them just as I have loved you and you will bring glory as
My love you share.

11/21/97

My Savior

When we see someone suffering, caught in life's despair,
The comfort God has given us we must then share.
When we respond in saving faith and to the Lord we submit,
We then put our lives in His hands to shape as He sees fit.

I know I can trust my Savior when I feel the world alarms,
Because there is no safer place than His loving arms.
I lift my heart to heaven to the loving and kind father there,
Waiting to release comfort in the silent communion of prayer.

I am a soldier of the Cross, a flower of the Lamb,
I will not fear to own my cross, a child of His I am.
Thank you, father, for Your spirit filing me with Your love and
Your power,
Changing me into Christ's image day by day and hour by hour.

To share in God's saving truth … we play a crucial part,
Because God is the only one who can transform a person's heart.
… Use what God has given you, do not count its worth so small,
God does not ask great things of you … faithfulness, that's all.
… He is seeking my gold to refine,
So I humbly trust Him, because my Savior is divine.

10/13/98

A Servant

Even tho' it cannot be said in one line or two.
God has bless me to share another poem with you.
I have come into the life of Jesus—He is my Lord and my friend.

His power flows through me … this message I now extend.
Lord, help me know from day to day the work I must carry through.
Grant me the wisdom to discern the things You would have me do.

I know all things work out for good, because it is in Your design.
Yet, You order my steps in Your Word for purposes divine.
… It is God's will that we read His Word from day to day.

Not just for knowledge, but much more … to love Him and to obey.
That is why I walk in faith and no foe or storm will I fear.
Because in His Word I am safe and He is always near.

Yes, gaining knowledge of God's Word can be a worthy goal.
Especially when it leads us to Him so He can nourish the soul.
If darkness is around me and earthly joys are flown.

God whispers His promise, never to leave me along.
… Physical eyes may not always see the work God is doing today.
But hope in His Word will bear fruit, even though there may be a delay.

One may be blessed with riches and rich in deeds.
God wants us to be generous when meeting other people's needs.
Therefore, we should give up sinful pride and take on a servant's role.

Then we will know Christ as a wellspring in the soul.
So let's work hard until He comes back and He will reward us then.
Because He promised to return, but we do not know when.

11/16/09

Our Love

When two people find with each other new beauty in
everyday living,
They open their hearts to each other by trusting, sharing, and
giving.

When two people share with each other a world of contentment
and fun,
They know they were meant for each other and two
people are truly one.

It is wonderful having someone to love when the
weather is sunny and bright,
And someone to share life's adventure and joy when
everything is just right.

When you cannot see your way through the problems
you face no matter how hard you try,
Real love comes through on the dark gloomy days
when the storm clouds take over the sky.

Real love makes the rough times less trouble to face
and every pleasure more fun,
Because it brings a peaceful fulfillment that will remain
through the shadows and sun.

When things were not going to smoothly, I remembered all the good times with you,
Because our love held a wonderful strength we could
count on to carry us though.

No matter what happens or what may come to be,
I thank God for letting me see the sunshine, because
you are standing beside me.

8/28/02

Paul and I as One

When I look back over my life I really could boast.
About the things that really helped me the most.
Sometimes I feel like the Apostle Paul, throughout his life he went through it all.

Even though his life was full of problems and despair.
Bear with me and I will share, in the early days Paul was not a believer.
After becoming an apostle he became a healer.
Paul boasted about things that really changed his life.
Yet we idolize things that bring us sugar and spice.
Paul talked about the time he spent in jail.
And his nights on the sea fighting a whale.
I can relate to Paul and his incarceration.

Especially when I look back at my life and see the revelation.
I could boast about the bad things that happened to me.
And the peace I felt when I told the Devil to flee.
At one time in my life I let many hours tick off the clock.
... When I gave my time and money for that ten dollar rock.
Even though my life was miserable as hell.
I was content during the time I spent in jail.

Some people wasted their time worrying about their release.
As for me, I love to remember every moment of inner peace.
If I must boast, let me boast about what God has done.
On how He gave eternal life through His only son.

Yes, the story of Paul strikes even my nerve.
Because when we live for the Devil, we get what we deserve.
Without the Apostle Paul, I could not tell this story.
That is why … to this day … I give God all the praise, honor, and glory.

9/1/96
—by Kevin Goff

www.ingramcontent.com/pod-product-compliance
Lightning Source LLC
LaVergne TN
LVHW050943080826
845145LV00004B/1397

* 9 7 8 0 9 8 2 4 2 9 2 5 9 *